To: ______________________________

From: ______________________________

Baptized on: ______________________________

For Pauline, my lovely sister, in memory of a sunny afternoon when we held hands, stepped into the River Jordan, and remembered our baptism.
I love you.
—Glenys

To Walid. Thank you for the adventure of a lifetime.
— Anna Kazimi

ZONDERKIDZ

*Baptized in the Water*


Requests for information should be addressed to:
Zonderkidz, 3900 *Sparks Dr. SE, Grand Rapids, Michigan 49546*

ISBN 978-0-310-73413-0 (hardcover)
ISBN 978-0-310-73414-7 (ebook)

---

Library of Congress Cataloging-in-Publication Data
Names: Nellist, Glenys, 1959- author. | Kazimi, Anna, illustrator.
Title: Baptized in the water: becoming a member of God's family / written by Glenys Nellist; illustrated by Anna Kazimi.
Description: Grand Rapids: Zonderkidz, 2022. | Audience: Ages 4–8 |
Summary: "Reading about baptism can help children understand how, through baptism, we become members of God's great family. Baptized in the Water, written by bestselling author Glenys Nellist, is a beautifully illustrated picture book that celebrates that very important event, no matter when or what form baptism takes in a person's life.
Baptized in the Water: Becoming a Member of God's Family: features beautiful prose and poetry that celebrates and explains baptism; illustrates various forms of baptism, from infant to adult; and showcases various Christian faith traditions through vibrant illustrations"—Provided by publisher.
Identifiers: LCCN 2021040757 (print) | LCCN 2021040758 (ebook) | ISBN 9780310734130 (hardcover) | ISBN 9780310734147 (ebook)
Subjects: LCSH: Baptism—Juvenile literature.
Classification: LCC BV811.3 .N45 2022 (print) | LCC BV811.3 (ebook) | DDC 231/.161—dc23/eng/20211021
LC record available at https://lccn.loc.gov/2021040757

LC ebook record available at https://lccn.loc.gov/2021040758



Cover Design: Kris Nelson
Illustrations: Ana Kazimi
Interior Design: Mallory Collins

*Printed in Malaysia*

---

22 23 24 25 IMG 10 9 8 7 6 5 4 3 2 1

# Baptized in the Water

## Becoming a Member of God's Family

Written by Glenys Nellist
Illustrated by Anna Kazimi

ZONDERkidz

Baptism is a beautiful, holy, mysterious gift. When water is poured on a person, when prayers are said, when songs are sung, and promises are made, God's holy, invisible Spirit hovers in the air . . . just like it did over two thousand years ago when Jesus stepped into the waters of the River Jordan. That wonderful day, Jesus was baptized by a man called John. And something amazing happened . . .

The heavens opened above, a white dove flew gently down, and God said, "This is my Son. I am pleased with him."

Can you imagine God smiling that day?

Baptized in the water,
Dove flies from above.
Jesus in the river,
Covered in God's love.

Ever since Jesus was baptized, Christians all around the world have chosen to be baptized too. And every time a baptism happens, God smiles and whispers, “This is my son. This is my daughter. I am pleased with them.”

When we are baptized, it’s a sign that we are part of God’s great family. There are different ways to be baptized, but the meaning is the same: in baptism we belong to God. The water makes us clean and new.

Baptized in the water,
A gift for me and you.
A sign that we belong to God,
Who makes us clean and new.

Sometimes parents bring their babies to church to be baptized. They want everyone to know that their child belongs to God. The pastor sprinkles or pours water on the baby's head, and everyone promises to love that little one, and teach him or her about God. The baby will not remember that special day, but the parents will never forget it!

Baptized in the water,
We promise, sing, and pray.
A little one's brought forward,
It's Baby's special day!

Sometimes older children or adults decide themselves they'd like to be baptized. They might go right under the water! They want everyone to know that they belong to God.

Baptized in the water,
Like Jesus long ago.
God's Holy Spirit dances,
As waters gently flow.

But you don’t need to be baptized in a church. Some people are baptized in a river, like Jesus was, or in a lake or even in an ocean!

Baptized in the water,
Gathered by the lake.
God hears our songs and prayers,
Each promise that we make.

No matter *where* we are
baptized—in a church

or a lake
or a river—

what matters is that
we are joined in one
human family,

and each of us
belongs to God.

**Baptized in the water,**
**Held in God's great care.**
**One family joined together,**
**Young and old, everywhere.**

No matter *how* we are baptized—whether we're covered by the water, or it's sprinkled or poured, what really matters is that we're covered in God's great love and grace.

When we are baptized, God's love pours over us, just like the water. God smiles and whispers, "You are my son. You are my daughter. I am pleased with you."

Baptized in the water,
Covered by God's grace.
We are God's sons and daughters,
In every time and place.

A Baptism Prayer

Dear God, thank you for the meaning and mystery of baptism. Thank you that when we are touched by water in baptism, you reach down to cover us with grace and hold us in your love. Remind us that through the gift of baptism we are one family, joined together around the world, across the years, by one Spirit, one faith, and one hope. We are your sons and daughters. We belong to you.

Amen.

There is one body and one Spirit, just as you were called to one hope when you were called; one Lord, one faith, one baptism.

Ephesians 4:4–5